Frontiers, Borderlands, Wests

AMERICAN HISTORY NOW

Series edited by Eric Foner and Lisa McGirr

Other titles in the series:

**SQUARING THE CIRCLES:
THE REACH OF COLONIAL AMERICA**
- Alan Taylor

**AMERICAN REVOLUTION
AND EARLY REPUBLIC**
- Woody Holton

JACKSONIAN AMERICA
- Seth Rockman

**SLAVERY, THE CIVIL WAR,
AND RECONSTRUCTION**
- Adam Rothman

**THE POSSIBILITIES OF POLITICS:
DEMOCRACY IN AMERICA,
1877 TO 1917**
- Robert D. Johnston

THE INTERWAR YEARS
- Lisa McGirr

**THE UNCERTAIN FUTURE OF AMERICAN
POLITICS, 1940 TO 1973**
- Meg Jacobs

1973 TO THE PRESENT
- Kim Phillips-Fein

THE UNITED STATES IN THE WORLD
- Erez Manela

THE "CULTURAL TURN"
- Lawrence B. Glickman

AMERICAN RELGION
- John T. McGreevy

ENVIRONMENTAL HISTORY
- Sarah T. Phillips

HISTORY OF AMERICAN CAPITALISM
- Sven Beckert

WOMEN'S AND GENDER HISTORY
- Rebecca Edwards

IMMIGRATION AND ETHNIC HISTORY
- Mae M. Ngai

**AMERICAN INDIANS AND THE STUDY
OF U.S. HISTORY**
- Ned Blackhawk

AFRICAN-AMERICAN HISTORY
- Kevin Gaines

To purchase these and other titles,
visit the American Historical Association's online store at
www.historians.org/pubshop

American History Now

Frontiers, Borderlands, Wests

By
Stephen Aron

With a foreword by **Eric Foner** and **Lisa McGirr**, series editors

American Historical Association
400 A Street, SE
Washington, DC 20003
www.historians.org

STEPHEN ARON is professor of history at University of California at Los Angeles, and executive director of the Institute for the Study of the American West at the Autry National Center. He is currently writing a book with the working title *Can We All Just Get Along: An Alternative History of the American West.*

COVER DESIGN AND LAYOUT: Chris Hale

© 2012 by the American Historical Association
ISBN: 978-0-87229-192-8

All rights reserved. No part of this book may be reproduced in any form without permission in writing from the publisher, except by a reviewer who wishes to quote brief passages in connection with a review written for inclusion in a magazine or newspaper.

Published in 2012 by the American Historical Association. As publisher, the American Historical Association does not adopt official views on any field of history and does not necessarily agree or disagree with the views expressed in this book.

This essay originally appeared in *American History Now* (ISBN 978-1-4399-0243-1), published by Temple University Press as part of the series Critical Perspectives on the Past, edited by Susan Porter Benson, Stephen Brier, and the late Roy Rosenzweig.

Library of Congress Cataloging-in-Publication data:

Aron, Stephen.

Frontiers, borderlands, Wests / by Stephen Aron; with a foreword by Eric Foner and Lisa McGirr.

p. cm. — (American history now)

Includes bibliographical references.

ISBN 978-0-87229-192-8

1. West (U.S.)—Historiography. I. Title.

F591.A76 2012

911.78—dc23   2012018648

Table of Contents

Series Foreword vi
Introduction 1
Revising and Reviving Terms 3
The Deeper Past Recast 8
The West "Belongs to All of Us" 14
Bibiliography 19

Series Foreword

First published in 1990, followed by a revised and expanded edition seven years later, *The New American History* introduced a generation of students, teachers, and members of the broader public to the ongoing transformation of the study of the American past. In the early twenty-first century, that transformation has continued apace. In embarking on a third edition, the editors decided to assemble an entirely new collection. First, we expanded the number of essays to eighteen, to allow us to incorporate emerging subfields not represented in the original editions. Second, we invited an entirely new group of historians to contribute. Each of the essays that follow is written by a young scholar at the forefront of current trends in his or her area of expertise. Eight deal with a specific time period, beginning with the colonial era; the remainder assess recent developments in historians' understanding of a major theme in the nation's past. To signal these substantive and generational changes, we gave the volume the new title *American History Now*.

It is worth noting at the outset that we have made no attempt to impose a uniform outlook or single interpretation on the contributors. We have given each author a free hand in defining his or her subject and developing an approach to it. Inevitably, therefore, there are overlaps, especially between chronological and thematic essays, as well as differences in emphasis and outlook. Nonetheless, certain themes recur with remarkable regularity.

The first editions of *The New American History* demonstrated, above all, the impact of the "new social history" on our understanding of the American past. Inspired initially by the social movements of the 1960s and 1970s, and influenced by methods and insights borrowed from other disciplines and from scholars of other national histories, American historians redefined the cast of characters who made up the nation's past. They devoted their energies to recovering the experience of previously neglected groups, not simply as an addition to a preexisting body of knowledge but as a fundamental redefinition of history itself. In the wake of that explosion of scholarship, our understanding of American history past was enormously enriched and expanded.

The scholars in this new edition build upon the work of that generation. Rather than seeking to debunk the interpretations of their forebears, these younger historians begin with the assumption that no narrative of American history can be considered complete that ignores the political, social, and cultural experiences of ordinary Americans and that fails to take into account the remarkable diversity that has always characterized American society. But they push this insight in dramatic new directions.

As these essays show, today's leading historians are less interested in developing new subfields or framing either/or dichotomies than in locating intersections and interactions. Categories like race and gender, touchstones of the new social history, are now considered essential to understanding major themes in American development, including the law, diplomacy, and public policy, rather than being limited to relations between blacks and whites or men and women. The distinction between "high" politics and that of ordinary folk has been jettisoned in favor of the study of the broad public sphere, defined so as to encompass many groups who were traditionally excluded from electoral participation yet who engaged in boisterous debates over issues such as economic justice and gender equality. Even national boundaries no longer delimit American history, as evidenced by the number of essays that touch on the history of "borderlands" where various national groups came into contact, as well as on the widespread interest in the global reach of the American experience. An age of globalization seems to demand embedding American history more powerfully than ever in a global framework.

One preoccupation of this new generation of scholars has been to link or reconnect previously fragmented studies of a diverse cast of characters into a new kind of synthesis, one quite different from the old "master narrative" in offering a richer and more complex view of the American past. The chronological essays, for example, devote attention to the importance of elites, established institutions, and public policy, but also place a strong emphasis on how less prominent groups responded to, and affected, constellations of power in the past. Women, Native Americans, workers, slaves, and others appear as important historical actors whose claims contested the shape of power relations. Some essays, like Woody Holton's on the revolutionary era, pointedly depart from the popular fascination with the founding fathers to emphasize the struggles of a broad array of distinct social groups. Others, including Seth Rockman's on the Jacksonian era, Robert Johnston's on Progressive America, and Kim Phillips-Fein's on the years since 1973, emphasize both national authority and the democratic aspirations of less powerful groups.

One theme of the essays that follow is the blurring of previously established scholarly boundaries, as subfields are redefined or abandoned in favor of broader new categories. The new history of capitalism, discussed by Sven Beckert, brings together older subfields such as labor history, business history, and economic history, all within a transnational framework. This new scholarship denaturalizes capitalism by making its emergence a subject of investigation rather than the result of some natural law standing outside of history. Environmental history, an emerging field mapped by Sarah

Phillips, investigates human interactions with the natural universe and the conflicts in politics, society, economics, and the world of ideas over the relationship between human and nonhuman. Diplomatic history, as Erez Manela shows, has been revitalized by incorporating insights from cultural history and benefiting from the "transnational turn." The study of America in the world now includes not simply diplomacy but the activities of nongovernmental actors as well, from performing artists to missionaries and auto salesmen. Mae Ngai charts the recent remaking of immigration history from a field focused on the "assimilation" of European newcomers to a new emphasis on circular worldwide patterns of migration and concepts of cultural diaspora and hybridity. These essays offer vivid examples of what Lawrence Glickman describes as the broader "cultural turn" in historical analysis, which in the past generation has affected virtually every aspect of American history. Cultural historians seek to understand the evolution and hidden power relations within categories—race, class, and so on—that previous scholars took for granted.

Some of the essays cover fields that were ignored in previous editions but have emerged at the forefront of current scholarship. As John McGreevy points out, historians have long neglected the powerful impact of religious faith and religious institutions in the nation's past, but today, thanks in part to the prominent role of religion in contemporary American society, these attract the attention of increasing numbers of historians. Native American history, as Ned Blackhawk delineates, has in recent years become a flourishing enterprise. As Blackhawk shows (and Alan Taylor's essay on the colonial era underscores), attention to the Native American experience profoundly reshapes our understanding of key moments in American history.

"The only obligation we have to history," Oscar Wilde once quipped, "is to rewrite it." There is nothing unusual or sinister in the fact that each generation rewrites history to suit its own needs. Taken together, these essays portray a field characterized by remarkable diversity, vitality, and open-mindedness. They suggest that at its best, the study of history remains a mode of collective self-discovery. This generation is well on the way to fashioning a history of the United States that transcends boundaries rather than reinforcing or reproducing them, that offers a candid appraisal of our own society's strengths and weaknesses while engaging in a mutually illuminating dialogue with the entire world.

Eric Foner
Lisa McGirr

"Americans have never had much use for histories," quipped historian Richard White, "but we do like anniversaries." For confirmation of White's aphorism, we need look no further than the hoopla surrounding the bicentennial of the Lewis and Clark expedition in 2004–2006. Commemorations included museum exhibitions, television documentaries, an Imax film, plays, musicals, and even an opera. Consumers could choose from an array of Lewis and Clark products, including Corps of Discovery cards and coins, "authentic" foods, puzzles, games, and action figures. The "LewisNClark" company marketed an array of gadgets for travelers. Scores of books appeared. There were Lewis and Clark cookbooks (presumably essential for those who purchase Lewis and Clark foods) and guidebooks (for wilderness enthusiasts eager to follow the Lewis and Clark Trail and put to use their LewisNClark gadgets). New biographies of the co-captains, the other members of the corps, and the Indians they encountered spilled off the shelves. Lest animal lovers feel left out, Lewis's dog, Seaman, was the subject of a couple of tomes. Two hundred years after Thomas Jefferson instructed Meriwether Lewis and William Clark to go forth "for the purposes of commerce," they fulfilled that part of their mission.

To be sure, the anniversary produced plenty of serious scholarship, some of which ran against the grain of bicentennial enthusiasm by questioning the success and significance of the expedition. Chief among the party crashers was Thomas Slaughter. In his *Exploring Lewis and Clark*, he deplored the excessive credit now given to a mission that had failed in most of its major objectives, was "irrelevant" to the subsequent history of American westward expansion, and was rightly forgotten for much of the nineteenth century.

The resurrection of Lewis and Clark occurred in the twentieth century, boosted, as several studies have pointed out, when the centennial of their journey coincided with World Fairs in St. Louis in 1904 and Portland in 1905. As presented in St. Louis and Portland, the Lewis and Clark expedition at one hundred looked very different than it did a century later, differences that speak to decisive shifts in the prevailing interpretations of the history of the American West. The expedition turned one hundred not long after Frederick Jackson Turner delivered his paper "The Significance of the Frontier in American History." Centennial commemorations celebrated along with Turner the victorious march of American expansion. By the Lewis and Clark bicentennial, however, the course of American expansion and empire no longer generated such good feelings, at least among the vast majority of academic historians. Instead, a "new western history," most fully framed in the texts of Patricia Nelson Limerick and Richard White, had come to the fore. This new western history made the ethnic diversity of the West its centerpiece. It also inverted Turner's triumphant progression into a tragic procession through a land scarred by the legacy of bloodsplattering, people-scattering, world-shattering conquests. All of which, its critics contended, left Americans not feeling good, but feeling guilty.

The latest round of Lewis and Clark remembrances reflected the impact of the new western history, promoting the Indian woman Sacagawea and Clark's African-American slave York to costarring roles and moving ecological concerns into the spotlight. Still, most bicentennial versions banished the darker vision of new western histories, emphasizing instead the amicable relations that Lewis and Clark fashioned with Indian peoples. Tellingly, the general public embraced the sunnier side of western history, even as a few scholars and a number of American Indians took issue with the ways in which the expedition had been turned into a tour of Kumbaya colonialism.

For the purposes of this survey of the field of western history, the shifting presentations and the most recent set of commemorations reveal much about changing interpretations of the history of the American West. Overrated though the expedition may be in the eyes of myth-breaking historians, tracking Lewis and Clark from centennial to bicentennial helps to distill the historiographic distance from Frederick Jackson Turner to Patricia Limerick and Richard White. Here, the connections between historical anniversaries that stimulate scholarship and heighten public awareness come clearly into view, as does the gap between what scholars deliver and what the public prefers.

In the last two decades, a number of anniversaries have similarly enlivened the field of western history and illuminated its evolutions. Along with the Lewis and Clark bicentennial, the quincentennial of Columbus's "discovery," the centennial of Turner's "frontier thesis," and the sesquicentennials of the Mexican-American War and California Gold Rush spoke to the concerns of western historians, and resulting publications speak to the currents of scholarship in the field. The productive inquiries these anniversaries generated show us how scholars have put new faces into the western past and changed the complexion of that history. We can take in the West, as historians have increasingly done, in overlapping subregional, regional, national, transnational, and international contexts. These anniversaries also prompted a rethinking of the chronologies we employ to divide the history of the West and the constructs we deploy to makes sense of it. Three terms—"frontier," "borderland," and "West" itself—have been instrumental to the history of the West, and each has been the subject of much debate in recent scholarship. In the case of all three, the plural form has become more proper, a revision with profound implications for how we comprehend what came before and after Lewis and Clark and for how we appraise the significance that frontiers, borderlands, and Wests hold for our histories.

REVISING AND REVIVING TERMS

Of all the recent anniversaries, the centennial of Frederick Jackson Turner's "The Significance of the Frontier in American History" least directly engaged a nonscholarly audience. Yet, it was this anniversary that sparked the most ardent debate among western historians. The arguments went to the heart of the field. At stake were the terms upon which the history of the American West had long been constructed and the terrain on which it played out.

Turner had first set those terms in an address to the fledgling American Historical Association in the summer of 1893. That conference, held in Chicago, also coincided with a grand world's fair, the Columbian Exposition, which was itself tied to a major historical anniversary, the quadricentennial of Christopher Columbus's discovery of the Americas. Challenging then-prevailing notions, Turner argued that the course of American development owed less to European foundations than to "American factors." What explained the course of American history and what distinguished Americans from Europeans was "the existence of an area of free land, its continuous recession, and the advance of American settlement westward." In the "colonization of the Great West," Turner claimed, could be found the seed of American democracy and the soil of American distinction.

Although Turner's talk went unnoticed by the millions of people who attended the nearby exposition, his frontier thesis soon became the most influential interpretation of American history; it would remain the reigning paradigm of western American history for a good part of the twentieth century. Key to Turner's framework was the concept of frontier, a word whose meaning Turner defined by making clear what it was not. It was "not the European frontier—a fortified boundary line running through dense populations." What it was Turner left more vague, or at least more varied: "the meeting point between savagery and civilization," "the hither edge of free land," "the Indian country and the outer margin of the 'settled area,'" "the line of most rapid and effective Americanization." Turner also differentiated between the frontier of the fur trader, the miner, the cattle raiser, and the farmer, though he discerned a recurring pattern in how these occupational stages filed across the continent. So while Turner assigned the word many meanings, recognized it to have several phases, and acknowledged numerous geographic chapters as it shifted westward, the essential repetition of the process of settlement and development unified the frontier experience, making it appropriate for Turner and his disciples to speak and write about *the American frontier*.

For Turner, the West, like the frontier, was hard to confine and thus difficult to define. Almost always when Turner referred specifically to "the West" in "The Significance of the Frontier in American History," he was discussing the lands between the Appalachian Mountains and the Mississippi River. Throughout that essay, he distinguished between "the West" and the "Far West," the region from the Mississippi to the Pacific, including the Louisiana Purchase and the territory through which Lewis and Clark traveled. In a subsequent volume published in 1906, Turner christened the region that encompassed the Ohio Valley and reached across to the west bank of the Mississippi "the New West." This, though, added to the confusion, for what Turner deemed the New West was, in regard to American occupation, older than the Far West, which Americans were coming to view nostalgically as the "Old West." But fixing boundaries and naming regions (or what he called sections) was not really Turner's objective. Sometimes, he erased the divisions between one West and another entirely, subsuming the parts under "the Great West," a nineteenth-century designation for the territory that stretched from the Appalachians to the Pacific. In fact, Turner's chief concern was not with "the West" but with westward expansion, with when, how, and to what effect the frontier had passed across the Great West.

The third vital construct, borderland, did not appear at all in Turner's most celebrated essay; its introduction into the lexicon of western historians came a few decades later in the work of Herbert Eugene Bolton. Bolton had briefly been a student of Turner, but he disputed his teacher's singular angle of vision. Where Turner made the westward march of Anglo-Americans the explanation for American development, Bolton maintained that the northward movement of the Spanish had also decisively shaped the colonization of the Great West. Dedicating much of his career to the study of "the Spanish borderlands" (the title of his seminal 1921 book on the subject), Bolton collected a trove of documents, published scores of books and articles, and sent hundreds of students to work in the field. In contrast to Turner's imprecision when it came to setting parameters, Bolton and his students were clearer about the limits of their terrain. In the "Boltonian" vision, the "Spanish Borderlands" extended to meet and attempted to defeat European imperial rivals' ambitions in western and southeastern North America, running principally across the lowest tier of the current states of the United States from California to Florida.

During the twentieth century, the study of the Spanish borderlands took hold at universities in that vast region, but the construct did not attain the national and popular reach of the frontier. Borderlands, by and large, remained an academic pursuit and a subfield of western history. By contrast, the frontier enjoyed a long run at the center of both academic inquiries and public understandings of American history. True, beginning during Turner's lifetime and intensifying after his death in 1932, scholars chipped away at the frontier edifice. By midcentury, most historians rejected the frontier as *the* explanation for American development. Lacking an alternative paradigm, historians of the American West were more reluctant to dismiss the frontier thesis, though this doggedness contributed to the disdain in which the field was held by more cutting-edge colleagues.

By the time the centennial of the "Significance of the Frontier" essay arrived in 1993, many western historians had separated themselves from Turner. Leading the charge was Patricia Limerick, whose 1987 book *The Legacy of Conquest* prodded western historians to finalize their divorce from Turner. The "f-word," she maintained, was "nationalistic and often racist (in essence, the area where white people get scarce)." Allegiance to it and to Turner trapped western historians in a nostalgic mythology that treated the West before its American colonization as "virgin land" in which the presence of Indian peoples mattered little. Adherence to the frontier also closed the western past at the passing of the frontier, which Turner, following the United States Census, dated to 1890. To confront the West's multiethnic past and its more recent history, Limerick urged western historians to abandon the outmoded, ethnocentric frontier concept and turn away from the process of westward expansion across the continent. In contrast with Turner, who put "the West" east of the Mississippi (at least for a time), Limerick and like-minded new western historians concentrated on the place that is the West today and set out to write its history as a region.

Demonstrating the possibilities of a regional approach, Richard White's 1991 textbook, *"It's Your Misfortune and None of My Own,"* surveyed the history of the American West without indexing the frontier of Frederick Jackson Turner. Further distancing his synthesis from Turner's notion that "the frontier was productive of individualism," White emphasized the essential role of the federal government in the making of the West. In turn, the West acted as the "kindergarten of the American state," for its exploration, conquest, colonization, economic development, and political incorporation required that the capacities of the national government be expanded. Dependence on (and resentment of) the federal government, White maintained, continued to shape the region through the twentieth century, an era to which *"It's Your Misfortune"* devoted almost half its pages.

If regionalists were ready to erase the frontier, they were less certain about where to place the West and what characteristics held it together. Clyde Milner wrote of the "psychological fault line" that separated westerners from other Americans, while Donald Worster, who identified aridity as the region's defining characteristic, described how his "bones" told him when he had entered the dry lands of the "true West." Aridity also led the editors of *The Atlas of the New West* to distinguish between the West and the West Coast, leaving the western parts of California, Oregon, and Washington beyond the region's boundaries. White settled on the northward bend of the Missouri River for his West's east and took the rest of the western United States in, but he conceded that the lines he drew around the region, on its east as well as on its north, south, and west, were "not naturally determined, they were politically determined." These borders, both internal and international, were just "a series of doors pretending to be walls." Ultimately, too, they made the West nothing more (or less) than what are now the western states of the United States. That seemed to shorten the West's history to the period after it became these (hence, the focus on the twentieth century), and it provided no grander explanation for regional coherence. Indeed, in a valuable collection of essays that examined subregional identities, editors David Wrobel and Michael Steiner concluded that "the West probably does have certain defining characteristics, but they are not readily and evenly applicable to all [its] parts." Better, perhaps, to acknowledge that there were and are "many Wests."

The hundredth anniversary of the frontier thesis roused a vigorous debate among western historians frequently characterized as pitting "place versus process." From the late 1980s through much of the 1990s, academic journals (and sometimes general newspapers and magazines) ran scores of articles that attacked or defended Turner and that disputed the merits of a place-based regional approach and a process-oriented frontier one. Against Limerick's indictment, an assortment of historians sought to salvage at least some of Turner's insights and to save the frontier, which they claimed was too deeply embedded in the public's consciousness to be jettisoned. Rather than a drastic amputation, a more surgical revision could remove the racist taint of a "meeting point between savagery and civilization" and leave the frontier more simply as a "meeting point," a cultural contact zone in which no single polity had established political hegemony.

This was the approach Robert Hine and John Mack Faragher chose for their 2000 survey *The American West: A New Interpretive History*. That text made frontier—or more accurately *frontiers* (which fittingly became the title of the 2007 brief edition of the book)—the foundation for their interpretation of a western history that, like Turner's, spanned the continent. Certainly, though,

Hine and Faragher's frontiers were not Turner's. In keeping with new trends in early American history (ably synthesized by Alan Taylor in his 2001 book *American Colonies*), Hine and Faragher adopted a polycolonial vision that decentered the Anglo-Americans' westward gaze. Comparing French, Spanish, and British colonial projects, Hine and Faragher highlighted how different were the frontiers that emerged between these newcomers and the diverse native people they encountered. In place of Turner's predictable procession from one social stage to the next, Hine and Faragher substituted a messier history of frontiers, which was especially attentive to the blending of ways that occurred where peoples met and mingled. To greater and lesser extents, "cultural fusion" characterized the various frontiers that Indians, Europeans, and Africans created across North America from the fifteenth to the nineteenth century, and it remained a hallmark of the West, with its entangled multiethnic population, through the twentieth century.

The fight between place and process produced no knockout blows, nor even a clear winner on points. As the centennial of Turner's "Significance of the Frontier" faded into the past, advocates for each side belatedly realized that the terms of their debate had been mischaracterized and had devolved into what David Hackett Fischer has described as the "fallacy of the false dichotomy." To be for place did not mean to be against process— and vice versa. Conquest, after all, was a process too. Moreover, as Hine and Faragher's text demonstrated, a focus on frontiers and earlier American Wests need not neglect the postfrontier history of the place that is now the West.

Amid the clamor about the frontier and the West in the 1980s and 1990s, what was happening to borderlands slipped by with less fanfare. To be sure, Bolton and the tradition of borderlands studies that he founded did not escape criticism from a new generation of scholars that derided the Euro centrism and "Hispanophilia" of Boltonians. These batterings, however, did not capture much attention outside the field, and, unlike opponents of Turner, critics of Bolton never suggested that the term "borderlands" be excised. Quite the contrary, they sought to expand the reach of the term and the terrain of the field. In this they succeeded spectacularly.

Here, too, a historical anniversary played a role. The sesquicentennial of the war between Mexico and the United States served as a reminder of how the southern boundary of the American West had been politically (really militarily) determined. It also acted as a stimulus to new scholarship, not just about the war, but about its impact on the peoples of the United States and Mexico. In that spirit, recent work has enlarged the geography of the borderlands to encompass the territories on both sides of the redrawn border. It has also extended the chronology. Where Bolton's borderlands closed with the collapse of the Spanish empire in the early nineteenth century, new studies pushed the borderlands construct to the present. And where Bolton and his disciples tended to spotlight the interests and actions of Europeans, scholars now accented the diversity and dynamism of borderland cultures.

In an even greater departure from earlier studies in the Boltonian tradition, it has become impossible to speak about "the" borderlands as denoting a single zone. In fact, scholars working far from the Mexico–U.S. line have unfurled the banner of borderlands. Indeed, in this era of globalization, borderlands seem to be everywhere. A perusal of recent literature turns up scores of books and articles that employ the construct of borderlands to interpret the histories of central and eastern Europe and the territories where Europe and Asia bleed together.

In the last few decades, not only has the concept gone global, but it has also become a catchall for any kind of border crossing. Thus the review of recent literature turns up explorations of "sexual borderlands" and "surfing borderlands" that seem a long way from Bolton's borderlands. The dangers of such promiscuous usages should be clear in light of the battles over frontier, which suggest a backlash against the "b-word" may be brewing—and perhaps before the 2021 centennial of the publication of Bolton's *The Spanish Borderlands*?

THE DEEPER PAST RECAST

While the Turner centennial and, to a lesser extent, the sesquicentennial of the Mexican-American War provoked debates that reworked the terms of western history and the terrain of the field, several other anniversaries served as principal agents for the recasting of that past. As noted, the Lewis and Clark bicentennial made stars of Sacagawea and York and made starkly apparent that the West they explored was no "virgin land." Even more dramatic for the repeopling and rewriting of histories of the West before Lewis and Clark was the fallout from the Columbian quincentennial. No anniversary changed public perceptions so deeply, principally by amplifying the voices and histories of Native Americans. This has also transformed scholarly interpretations, which now delve into pre-Columbian histories of North America, make the "Columbian exchange" the starting point for understanding the conquest and colonization of the continent, and take Indian power and prerogatives seriously in sorting the outcomes of imperial ventures in the centuries after 1492. For what happened after Lewis and Clark, the Gold Rush and the Golden State have taken a turn in the scholarly spotlight. To be sure, the sesquicentennial of the California Gold Rush lacked the public drama sparked by the Columbian quincentennial. But its scholarly impact has been considerable, reconfiguring the Gold Rush's place in nineteenth-century history and underscoring the significance of California to the history of the West and the nation. Before, during, and after the Gold Rush, as new scholarship has elaborated, the Golden State exemplified, magnified, and prefigured the history of the West. Taken together, these recastings have enlarged the company, extended the run, and altered the arc of western history.

Conspicuous as the changes were between the centennial and bicentennial interpretations of the Lewis and Clark expedition, this swing did not compare with the fall suffered by Christopher Columbus between 1892 and 1992. At the four hundredth anniversary, the Columbian Exposition made Columbus synonymous with progress and promise, and his champions in the Catholic Church campaigned for his canonization. A century later, big plans were announced for quincentennial celebrations, but almost all of these were canceled in the face of fierce opposition, the most aggrieved being American Indians. Rather than a candidate for sainthood or the avatar of human progress, protesters blamed Columbus for having ushered the genocide of Native Americans, the enslavement of Africans, and the destruction of the global environment. While scholarly treatments of Columbus did not hold him personally culpable for all the evils that ensued from his voyages, they, too, tarnished the Columbian legacy. The excavation of pre-Columbian histories has given us a better sense of the worlds we have lost. And the more we learn about the decimation of Indian peoples in the centuries after 1492, the more we grasp how European colonists in North America were, in John Murrin's phrase, the "beneficiaries of catastrophe."

The first impact of this scholarship on western history is to deepen its chronology. Not that long ago, western historians might commence their courses with Lewis and Clark or perhaps reach a couple of centuries back for a lecture or two on the Spanish exploration and invasion of lands north of Mexico. What came before the coming of Europeans was dismissed as "prehistory," with pre-Columbian Indians consigned to static worlds. No more, for recent scholarship has recovered a past filled with peoples in motion, societies in flux, cultures entangling, and polities expanding and contracting. Frontiers and borderlands, in short, did not await the arrival of Europeans, and pre-Columbian developments shaped the course of subsequent encounters with Europeans and Africans as much as did progress across the Atlantic.

Nothing in their prior histories, though, could prepare American Indians for the devastation wrought by imported diseases. Back in 1893, Turner had declared that "our early history is the study of European germs developing in an American environment." He did not realize how right he was, because the "germs" to which he referred were just a metaphor for the European ideas and institutions that were transplanted to and then transformed by the American frontier. But, as Alfred Crosby first elucidated in the 1970s, the microbes that Europeans brought with them proved deadly agents of conquest when unleashed upon people who lacked immunities to these diseases. In the years since Crosby first brought "virgin soil epidemics" into the Columbian conversation, historical demographers and epidemiologists have tussled over how large the pre-1492 census of the Americas was and how much of the decline after that should be attributed to diseases (as opposed to the demoralization that followed epidemics and the immiseration that accompanied European takeover of their lands). As Jared Diamond's 1997 best seller proclaimed, Indians also suffered because Europeans possessed guns and steel, and Indians did not before 1492. Yet it was germs, the middle element in Diamond's title, that should have been placed first. These precipitated the worst demographic calamity in human history, and these best explain why Europeans were able to conquer the Americas and where they were able to establish "neo-Europes."

Pathogens, Crosby recognized, were only part of the package of animals, plants, people, and products that passed between Old and New Worlds after 1492. Because so much of the flow of the first three moved from Europe and Africa to the Americas and because the "Columbian exchange" so clearly enabled the European exploitation and occupation of the Americas, Crosby labeled the process "ecological imperialism." But this did not mean that Indians reaped no benefit from the ecological invasion, as was most obvious in the interior grasslands of North America. There, the introduction of the horse and the spread of imported trade goods (including guns) enhanced the material cultures of Plains peoples and augmented the wealth and power of some of them.

Some, but not all. As works by Elliott West, Richard White, Colin Calloway, and Pekka Hamalainen have detailed, in the eighteenth century, many of those who were most enriched and empowered were newcomers to the grasslands. From different directions, the Cheyennes, the Lakotas, and the Comanches moved onto the Plains, where horses allowed them to hunt more bison, control more territory, and take captives from people with fewer horses and fewer guns. From James Brooks's *Captives and Cousins* and Ned Blackhawk's *Violence over the Land*, we have learned how far the dominoes from the "contested Plains" toppled, as those pushed off the grasslands turned their violence and captive taking against Great Basin peoples who had fewer (if any) horses and guns. Even among the Indians whom White characterized as the "winners of the West" in the eighteenth century, the unequal distribution of wealth (translated into horses and wives) meant that some Plains men won more than others. For Plains women, in general, the "equestrian revolution" brought more work (as more skins needed to be dressed) and less power (as the growing of crops, which had been women's domain, lost importance).

On the Plains and across the continent, taking the wealth and power of Indian societies seriously has remapped the history of post-Columbian North America. Again, not very long ago (and, in fact, still too often), American history textbooks typically featured maps that erased the presence of Indians and carved up the continent according to the claims of European powers. Based on imperial projections, such maps bore little relation to the actual situation on the ground in the seventeenth and eighteenth centuries. If British colonists gradually extended their exclusive occupation inland from the Atlantic coast, elsewhere most colonial settlements in North America existed as islands amid oceans of Indian countries. The presence and security of these enclaves and the fate of European empires rested on a variety of negotiated arrangements and cultural mixing with native peoples.

Richard White's enormously influential book *The Middle Ground* made famous (at least among academic historians) one such arrangement. Born, in this instance, of mutual weakness and fortuitous misunderstandings, White's middle ground was at once a diplomatic alliance fashioned by French and Algonquian Indians around the Great Lakes and a broader blurring of European and Indian ways. As his book detailed, the middle ground endured (if often tenuously) through much of the eighteenth century and extended (if often tentatively) around the Great Lakes and into the Ohio Valley.

The Middle Ground gave rise to middle grounds, as historians, following White, found (or claimed to find) similar intercultural compositions in other places at other times. Rather than a landscape dominated by Europeans, the "middle grounding" of early American history emphasized the power that native peoples exercised and their ability to compel accommodations from colonial intruders. This situation, Jeremy Adelman and I posited, most often emerged in the interior of the continent where the claims of European empires overlapped. In these borderlands during the eighteenth century, Indians successfully "played imperial rivals off against one another," a practice that allowed them to negotiate more favorable terms of trade and sustain more inclusive frontiers.

Beyond middle grounds, the latest western history has affirmed the existence and persistence of "native grounds," zones where Europeans remained subordinated to Indians. Consider, for example, eighteenth-century Texas, where, Juliana Barr has shown, Indians "dictated the rules and Europeans were the ones who had to accommodate, resist, and persevere." Barr's remapping of these colonial borderlands accented the centrality of gender to Texas Indians' constructions of power relations within and between societies. To be sure, Spanish and French intruders, with their preference for race-based classifications of difference, often misunderstood the alternative systems among the Indians they encountered. Yet, through a "diplomacy of gender," tentative truces and trade relations were established, and women, as captives, slaves, and emissaries, emerged as crucial brokers of the more enduring connections that took root in eighteenth-century Texas.

The apotheosis of Indian power was the "Comanche Empire," a designation that has as yet found its way onto few maps of colonial North America, but soon should, thanks to pathbreaking books by Pekka Hamalainen and Brian Delay. In giving his book that title, Hamalainen challenged the convention that reserved empire building to Europeans, at least north of Mexico. But as *The Comanche Empire* explicated, on the southern Plains "European imperialism not only stalled in the face of indigenous resistance, it was eclipsed by indigenous imperialism." "Comancheria" continued to expand well into the nineteenth century. As Delay has detailed, the raiding of Comanches (as well as Kiowas, Apaches, and Navajos) nearly depopulated parts of northern Mexico, weakened the inhabitants' attachment to the Mexican nation, and contributed to the loss of the territory to the United States. That territorial transfer came about in 1848 and included much of the Comanches' realm. But whether the United States would be able to restrain the "incursions" of Indians into Mexico, as required by Article 11 of the Treaty of Guadalupe Hidalgo, remained to be seen.

Included in the territorial handover from Mexico to the United States was California, where the discovery of gold that same year set off an unprecedented rush. One hundred fifty years later and in the decade since the sesquicentennial of the Gold Rush, California, which sometimes fell outside the new West's "true West," has regained its position in western history. California has been and remains "fundamentally western," in Walter Nugent's view, "at the edge of the West and at its center, all at once."

Like other histories in the era of the Columbian quincentennial, new California histories have sometimes simply inverted older understandings. Like Columbus, Father Junipero Serra has seen his reputation plummet. Once he and fellow missionaries were venerated for the souls they saved and the colony they opened; now the missionary regime has been recast as a reign of terror. More nuanced are the interpretations offered by James Sandos, Kent Lightfoot, and Steven Hackel, whose books demolish the former view that the Spaniards dominated California Indians completely. Instead, these studies detail how California Indians, like their counterparts to the east, rebuilt communities in the face of significant population declines and colonial demands. Within the missions, Indians and Spanish engaged one another on unequal terms, but even there Spanish authority depended on a stratum of native officials largely drawn from the ranks of traditional Indian leaders.

The economy, society, and culture of Mexican California have also received a makeover, often harsh, but one that has better connected the regime to broader developments across North America associated with the "market revolution." Albert Hurtado's illumination of the more "intimate frontiers" between men and women, for example, has pretty much drained the romance from oft-told tales of life in "Old California." In keeping with studies of interethnic mixing across the West, Hurtado's research has pointed out how marital and sexual unions both engraved and effaced boundaries between peoples. At the same time, Californios have taken on a more energetic and entrepreneurial face; works by Louise Pubols and David Igler have exhibited how landed elites seized opportunities for profit from commerce that increasingly crossed the Pacific and tied California into an emerging Pacific world system. These deepening trading ties and the migration of people before the Gold Rush from across the continent and across the Pacific made Mexican California in its final years a far more cosmopolitan place than contemporary Anglo-American observers and generations of historians appreciated. Nowhere was this cosmopolitanism better displayed than around the polyglot settlement of New Helvetia established by John Sutter (and featured in several of Hurtado's books).

It was, of course, the discovery of gold on land that Sutter claimed that truly opened the floodgates into California. The scale and global scope of this population movement dwarfed any previous migration to California or into the West, and its extremely unbalanced character—being almost entirely male—made the gold fields a fascinating laboratory in which to examine the collisions of cultures and the constructions of racial and gender relations. These, as Susan Johnson has uncovered, were closely related, for in the nearly all-male diggings, the reassessment of notions about gender and sexuality were entwined with ideas about race and ethnicity. In this and so many other ways, the California experience heralded developments in subsequent mining rushes. Indeed, a hallmark of scholarship that appeared around the sesquicentennial is its recognition that what happened in California did not stay in California. To that point, books by Malcolm Rohrbough, Brian Roberts, Yong Chen, and Aims McGuinness call attention to the impact of the Gold Rush on those left behind and on the places they passed through. Rohrbough and Roberts, in particular, stake the claim that the Gold Rush transformed the American nation more than any event in the first half of the nineteenth century, to which Leonard Richards would add that it was also a critical precipitant to the Civil War.

The connections between California, the West, and the nation grew even more pronounced after the Civil War, a period typically referred to as the Era of Reconstruction. Until relatively recently, historians of Reconstruction usually concentrated on the fate of freed people in the American South and closed their studies in 1877. Now, however, Reconstruction has taken on a broader meaning, a wider scope, and a longer chronology, with the West acknowledged as an integral component in the struggles to remake race relations, establish the primacy of the federal government, and consolidate an industrial capitalist order. No longer distracted by a handful of famous gunfights, historians have now more thoroughly exposed the ethnic and economic roots of most of the violence that occurred during what Richard Maxwell Brown has called the "western Civil War of incorporation." They have brought to light the devices by which forms of unfree labor persisted across the West long after the Civil War, as well as the biases and laws that sought to keep peoples apart—or at least put them in their place.

Chief among these place putters, and now a prime focus of scholarship about California, the West, and the United States, were the shifting boundaries of "whiteness." In the second half of the nineteenth century, the dynamics of whiteness exercised considerable control over the opportunities of life in California—over where individuals resided and worked, what they were paid, with whom they associated, and even whether they could enter California at all. For Mexicans, the shift seemed to push them out of the circle of those considered white. By contrast, the trajectory for European immigrants generally moved in the other direction, and, as the privileges of whiteness opened up to them, the roles and rights granted to Indians, Mexicans, Chinese, and African Americans narrowed. In California and the West, then, the postbellum reordering of race relations closed off countless opportunities. Still, reconstructions were ongoing, even if many breaches did not become visible until well into the twentieth century.

THE WEST "BELONGS TO ALL OF US"

One significant anniversary that went entirely unmarked and unremembered was the centennial of the 1903 movie *The Great Train Robbery*. Shot in New Jersey, that twelve-minute film gave birth to the genre that defined and dominated American cinema for a good part of the twentieth century. The thousands of westerns that followed *The Great Train Robbery* did more to shape public perceptions of the West and its history than any scholarly statement. Nor was the impact of westerns limited to the United States. Indeed, when the genre lost favor in Hollywood, foreigners revised and revived it. Most famous perhaps were the "Spaghetti westerns" of Italian director Sergio Leone, which were filmed in Spain, based on Japanese movies, and starred a cast of American, Italian, and Yugoslav actors. In Frayling's *Once Upon a Time in Italy*, Leone states, "the western belongs to all of us. . . . It belongs to the world now."

The lack of interest of western historians in the centennial of *The Great Train Robbery* comes as no surprise in light of scholarly trends. To be sure, historians continue to nod to the power of the "imagined West." At its simplest, this involves pointing out how images and representations from paintings, photography, dime novels, films, and television shows have distorted what really happened. More sophisticated are acknowledgments of the inseparability of "western myth" and western history. In fact, though, most historians pay only lip service to the West of the imagination, leaving its study and its ties to the history of the West to scholars in other disciplines. Notable anomalies include Martha Sandweiss's book on photography and the American West, which elucidates how the medium and the region developed together, and Louis Warren's biography of Buffalo Bill, which presents a compelling portrait of the person and the persona he (and others) created and of the culture in which the man and his myth operated. But these and a handful of other exceptions prove the rule identified by Ryan Carey and Flannery Burke: "Western historians tend to assert the intertwined nature of myth and reality more than they explore it."

While western historians have of late paid little heed to westerns, they have taken up Leone's maxim in other ways. First, they have made western history for all of us by being far more inclusive about who has made that history. Second, they have brought the history of the West to everyone by breaking through the barrier that the closing of the frontier once imposed. Rather than a history trapped "back then" (essentially ending one hundred plus years ago) or confined to places "out there" (meaning those parts of the West where its open spaces still endured), newer western histories have brought the past to the "here and now." Thus have the twentieth-century West and its urban "oases" gained primacy. Third, along with other American historians, western historians have adopted Leone's globalized lens, moving beyond the nation as the sole container in which to fit their histories. Instead, the latest scholarship has accented the transnational and international dimensions of western history and has explored the connections and comparisons that have linked the West to the world.

Through the nineteenth century, the frontiers and borderlands of North America were crossroads for people from diverse places at the intersections of nations and empires, but the worldliness of the West became even more evident during the twentieth century. Its resources were then pulled more deeply into the global economy and its population was further augmented by flows from afar. As Walter Nugent has pointed out, the number of homesteaders, a movement long associated with the 1862 act that encouraged settlement of the Great Plains in the late nineteenth century, did not actually peak until early in the twentieth century. Recent syntheses about the peopling of the West by Nugent and Elliott Barkan attend to this continuation and then the collapse of homesteading, while also explaining how and why the West remained a colossal magnet for both internal migrants and immigrants. To be sure, the magnetism was not spread equally across the region, and legal restrictions and extralegal pressures often redirected and for several decades interrupted the influx of foreigners. Nonetheless, nothing distinguishes the twentieth-century West or its new histories so much as the recognition of the region's demographic diversity. Absent this multiethnic complexion, the West, Richard White remarked, "might as well be New Jersey with mountains."

As in earlier times, the mix was a combustible one. Most of the conflicts that bedeviled the West during Reconstruction carried over into the twentieth century. As new books by Thomas Andrews and Katherine Benton-Cohen eloquently attest, the labor strife and eruptions of violence at Ludlow in 1914 and Bisbee in 1917 continued the struggles over racial boundaries and industrial capitalist supremacy that had characterized earlier chapters in the western war of incorporation.

The volume of newcomers, especially those moving north from Mexico during and after the Mexican Revolution, reshuffled the ethnic profile of the West in the twentieth century, particularly across the Southwest and in no place more dramatically than Los Angeles. Through the first third of the twentieth century, Los Angeles was the "whitest" of major American cities. That situation changed, however, when Mexican immigrants were joined by what James Gregory has called the "Southern Diaspora," which brought significant numbers of African Americans to California during and after World War II. A "second gold rush" was how Marilynn Johnson has described the impact of World War II on California, though in terms of ethnic diversity, the real tidal wave followed major immigration reform in 1965. That reopened Los Angeles, California, and the West to substantial immigration from Asia, which together with ongoing immigration from Mexico and Central America, thoroughly changed the demographic complexion of Los Angeles by century's end—as it has the rest of the nation. In fact, at the start of the twenty-first century, New Jersey, now boasting growing Latin American and Asian American populations, has come to look more like the West—though still without the mountains.

Destructive riots in Los Angeles in 1965 and 1992 showed that race relations remained a trigger for violence in the incorporated West, much as it had been in the incorporating one. Historians of Los Angeles and other western cities have probed these urban conflagrations, the most prescient and darkest account being Mike Davis's *City of Quartz*. More surprising and certainly more uplifting are studies by Scott Kurashige, George Sanchez, Allison Varzally, and Mark Wild that revisited Los Angeles's multiethnic neighborhoods in the middle decades of the twentieth century and recovered social networks fashioned in streets, shops, and schools that, to borrow Varzally's phrase, "colored" across ethnic lines. From these associations, at first fleeting and fragile, these authors have traced the emergence of more lasting bonds that translated into joint political action. In Los Angeles and across the region, struggles for civil rights and efforts to undo the legal privileges afforded to whiteness ended up taking many forms and brought together shifting coalitions, but at bottom all shared the premise that the American West belongs to everyone who lives there.

For Leone, the "we" in "West" was wider still, taking in not only all who lived there but also all who imagined themselves there. Admittedly, historians have not done much of late for the latter category of inhabitants. They have, however, been actively engaged in bringing the history of the West into conversation with the rest of the world. For western historians, this global turn has meant a further renunciation of the legacy of Frederick Jackson Turner. Turner, after all, had encouraged American historians to look away from foreign "germs" and focus on the frontier, where, he contended, the "really American" part of American history was to be found. Yet historians have now recast the frontiers of North America as multinational before they became national and have determined that the West, even after its incorporation into the United States, continued to be decisively shaped by immigrant chains and commodity flows that moved across borders and oceans.

By no means is this global turn an entirely new development. Threequarters of a century ago, Herbert Bolton devoted his presidential address to the American Historical Association to a call for an "epic of greater America" that would cultivate a common and comparative history of the Americas. Few, however, answered Bolton's call, and parallel efforts to build "comparative frontiers" into a vibrant field also languished—until recently, when suddenly transnational connections and global comparisons emerged as a signature of the newest western histories.

Fittingly, historians of borderlands have taken the lead. The border provides an ideal vantage point to assess the power of empires and nationstates to enforce territorial claims, while also exposing the limits of that power at the periphery. The border is the place, in Elliott Young's words, where "the nation continues to be made, but it is also the place where it is unmade." The latter fact has especially impressed itself in recent studies, which have emphasized the permeability of borders and the weakness of empires and nation-states at their perimeters. What has become most obvious to historians of borderlands is the necessity of crossing borders. Understanding what happened on one side requires knowing what occurred on the other, and it also now increasingly entails research in archives on both sides of the border. A sterling example of this is Kelly Lytle Hernandez's history of the U.S. Border Patrol, which uses both American and Mexican sources to recover the confrontations and collaborations between American and Mexican officials that together shaped the policing of people moving across the U.S.-Mexico border.

In the spirit of Bolton's "Epic of Greater America," historians of borderlands have also taken on comparative projects. Because the concept of borderlands has gone global, there is now much to compare. Within North America, the boundary between the United States and Canada has received much less attention than the line between the United States and Mexico, but a collection of essays edited by Benjamin Johnson and Andrew Graybill opens a stimulating discussion about the similarities and differences between those borders and the borderlands that surround them.

Comparisons tend to unsettle assumptions about American exceptionalism, and, in the particular case of western American history, they often invoke discomforting parallels. Around the time of the Columbian quincentennial, protesters talked of "genocide" and "holocaust" to capture the correspondences between the extermination of American Indians and European Jews. For the most part, historians employed these words more cautiously, maintaining a distinction between the unwitting spread of diseases and the deliberate, state-sponsored eradications pursued by the Nazis. But the terms that have lately gained favor among western historians are hardly more comforting. John Mack Faragher and Gary Anderson, for example, have borrowed the concept of "ethnic cleansing," which was invented in the 1990s to describe the contemporary horrors in the Balkans, and applied it to the deliberate, state-sponsored expulsion of French Acadians and Texas Indians from their respective homelands. Historians have also increasingly used the lens of colonialism or, more specifically, "settler colonialism" to set expansion across North America in a worldwide framework and to bring insights from similar situations into the newest histories of the West.

As an example of "ethnic cleansing" and "settler colonialism," the history of the West has come a long way from the triumphant trail of Frederick Jackson Turner's frontier and the good feelings of the Lewis and Clark bicentennial. The view gets even nastier when we consider who drew inspiration from the American model of spatial expansion and economic development. As Charles Bright and Michael Geyer have pointed out, in the twentieth century the most obvious candidates were the Germans and the Japanese, who "imagined themselves doing in the twentieth century what they thought Americans had done in the nineteenth: conquering a territorial hinterland" while purging it of "savage inhabitants" to transform it into "a source of food and resources, a controllable inland market, and a homeland for a growing population organized for maximum production."

We should beware, however, of allowing our perspective on westward expansion and its aftermath to go too far or too exclusively to the dark side. As the bicentennial celebrated (sometimes excessively), Lewis and Clark did generally get along with the Indians they encountered. Moreover, from middle grounds in the eighteenth century to multiethnic neighborhoods in the twentieth, historians have recovered episodes of concord, times and places in which people overcame their differences, at least temporarily, as opposed to being overcome by them. These, too, are part of the history of frontiers, borderlands, and Wests, and they at least suggest that the West could and still might belong to all of us.

BIBILIOGRAPHY

Abbott, Carl. *Frontiers Past and Future: Science Fiction and the American West.* Lawrence: University Press of Kansas, 2006.

———. *How Cities Won the West: Four Centuries of Urban Change in Western North America.* Albuquerque: University of New Mexico Press, 2008.

Adelman, Jeremy, and Stephen Aron. "From Borderlands to Borders: Empires, Nation-States, and the Peoples in Between in North American History." *American Historical Review* 104 (June 1999): 814–841.

Anderson, Gary. *The Conquest of Texas: Ethnic Cleansing in the Promised Land, 1820–1875.* Norman: University of Oklahoma Press, 2005.

Andrews, Thomas. *Killing for Coal: America's Deadliest Labor War.* Cambridge, MA: Harvard University Press, 2008.

Aron, Stephen. *American Confluence: The Missouri Frontier from Borderland to Border State.* Bloomington: Indiana University Press, 2006.

Avila, Eric. *Popular Culture in the Age of White Flight: Fear and Fantasy in Suburban Los Angeles.* Berkeley: University of California Press, 2004.

Barkan, Elliott. *From All Points: America's Immigrant West, 1870–1952.* Bloomington: Indiana University Press, 2007.

Barr, Juliana. *Peace Came in the Form of a Woman: Indians and Spaniards in the Texas Borderlands.* Chapel Hill: University of North Carolina Press, 2007.

Benton-Cohen, Katherine. *Borderline Americans: Racial Division and Labor War in the Arizona Borderlands.* Cambridge, MA: Harvard University Press, 2009.

Blackhawk, Ned. *Violence over the Land: Indians and Empires in the Early American West.* Cambridge, MA: Harvard University Press, 2006.

Blodgett, Peter J. *Land of Golden Dreams: California in the Gold Rush Decade, 1848–1858.* San Marino, CA: Huntington Library Press, 1999.

Bogue, Allan G. *Frederick Jackson Turner: Strange Roads Going Down.* Norman: University of Oklahoma Press, 1998.

Bolton, Herbert E. "The Epic of Greater America," *American Historical Review,* 38 (April 1933): 448–474.

———. *The Spanish Borderlands: A Chronicle of Old Florida and the Southwest.* New Haven, CT: Yale University Press, 1921.

Bowes, John. *Exiles and Pioneers: Eastern Indians in the Trans-Mississippi West.* New York: Cambridge University Press, 2007.

Bright, Charles, and Michael Geyer. "Where in the World Is America? The History of the United States in the Global Age." In Thomas Bender, ed., *Rethinking American History in a Global Age,* 63–99. Berkeley: University of California Press, 2002.

Brooks, James. *Captives and Cousins: Slavery, Kinship, and Community in the Southwest Borderlands.* Chapel Hill: University of North Carolina Press, 2002.

Brown, Richard Maxwell. *No Duty to Retreat: Violence and Values in American History and Society.* New York: Oxford University Press, 1991.

Burke, Flannery. *From Greenwich Village to Taos: Primitivism and Place at Mabel Dodge Luhan's.* Lawrence: University Press of Kansas, 2008.

Calloway, Colin G. *One Vast Winter Count: The Native American West before Lewis and Clark.* Lincoln: University of Nebraska Press, 2003.

Carey, Ryan, and Flannery Burke. "Corralling the Real and Imagined West: A Review Essay." Unpublished paper presented to Autry Western History Workshop, 2003.

Cayton, Andrew, and Fredrika Tuete, eds. *Contact Points: American Frontiers from the Mohawk Valley to the Mississippi, 1750–1830*. Chapel Hill: University of North Carolina Press, 1998.

Chan, Sucheng, ed. *Chinese American Transnationalism: The Flow of People, Resources, and Ideas between China and America during the Chinese Exclusion Era*. Philadelphia: Temple University Press, 2006.

Chavez, John R. *Beyond Nations: Evolving Homelands in the North Atlantic World, 1400–2000*. New York: Cambridge University Press, 2009.

Chavez-Garcia, Miroslava. *Negotiating Conquest: Gender and Power in California, 1770–1880*. Tucson: University of Arizona Press, 2004.

Chen, Yong. *Chinese San Francisco 1850–1943: A Transpacific Community*. Stanford, CA: Stanford University Press, 2000.

Cronon, William. *Nature's Metropolis: Chicago and the Great West*. New York: W. W. Norton, 1991.

Cronon, William, George Miles, and Jay Gitlin, eds. *Under an Open Sky: Rethinking America's Western Past*. New York: W. W. Norton, 1992.

Crosby, Alfred W., Jr. *The Columbian Exchange: Biological and Cultural Consequences of 1492*. Westport, CT: Greenwood Press, 1972.

———. *Ecological Imperialism: The Biological Expansion of Europe, 900–1900*. New York: Cambridge University Press, 1986.

Culver, Lawrence. *The Frontier of Leisure: Southern California and the Shaping of Modern America*. New York: Oxford University Press, 2010.

Davis, Mike. *City of Quartz: Excavating the Future in Los Angeles*. London: Verso, 1990.

Delay, Brian. *War of a Thousand Deserts: Indian Raids and the U.S.-Mexican War*. New Haven, CT: Yale University Press, 2008.

Deloria, Philip J. *Indians in Unexpected Places*. Lawrence: University Press of Kansas, 2004.

Deverell, William, ed. *A Companion to the American West*. Boston: Blackwell, 2004.

———. *Whitewashed Adobe: The Rise of Los Angeles and the Remaking of Its Mexican Past*. Berkeley: University of California Press, 2004.

Deverell, William, and David Igler, eds. *A Companion to California History*. Boston: Blackwell, 2008.

Diamond, Jared. *Guns, Germs, and Steel: The Fates of Human Societies*. New York: W. W. Norton, 1997.

DuVal, Kathleen. *The Native Ground: Indians and Colonists in the Heart of the Continent.* Philadelphia: University of Pennsylvania Press, 2006.

Elliott, J. H. *Empires of the Atlantic World: Britain and Spain in America, 1492–1830.* New Haven, CT: Yale University Press, 2006.

Faragher, John Mack. *A Great and Noble Scheme: The Tragic Story of the Expulsion of the French Acadians from Their American Homeland.* New York: W. W. Norton, 2005.

Fischer, David Hackett. *Historians' Fallacies: Toward a Logic of Historical Thought.* New York: Harper & Row, 1970.

Flores, Dan L. *The Natural West: Environmental History in the Great Plains and Rocky Mountains.* Norman: University of Oklahoma Press, 2001.

Foley, Neil. *The White Scourge: Mexican, Blacks, and Poor Whites in Texas Cotton Culture.* Berkeley: University of California Press, 1997.

Frayling, Christopher. *Once Upon a Time in Italy: The Westerns of Sergio Leone.* New York: Harry N. Abrams, 2005.

Fresonke, Kris, and Mark Spence, eds. *Lewis and Clark: Legacies, Memories, and New Perspectives.* Berkeley: University of California Press, 2004.

Furstenberg, Francois. "The Significance of the Trans-Appalachian Frontier in Atlantic History." *American Historical Review* 113 June 2008): 647–677.

Gordon, Linda. *Dorothea Lange: A Life beyond Limits.* New York: W. W. Norton, 2009.

———. *The Great Arizona Orphan Abduction.* Cambridge, MA: Harvard University Press, 1999.

Graybill, Andrew. *Policing the Plains: Rangers, Mounties, and the North American Frontier, 1875–1910.* Lincoln: University of Nebraska Press, 2007.

Greenberg, Amy. *Manifest Manhood and the Antebellum American Empire.* New York: Cambridge University Press, 2005.

Gregory, James N. *The Southern Diaspora: How the Great Migrations of Black and White Southerners Transformed America.* Chapel Hill: University of North Carolina Press, 2005.

Grossman, James, ed. *The Frontier in American Culture.* Berkeley: University of California Press, 1994.

Gutierrez, David. *Walls and Mirrors: Mexican Americans, Mexican Immigrants, and the Politics of Ethnicity.* Berkeley: University of California Press, 1995.

Gutierrez, Ramon. *When Jesus Came, the Corn Mothers Went Away: Marriage, Sexuality, and Power in New Mexico, 1500–1846*. Stanford, CA: Stanford University Press, 1991.

Gutierrez, Ramon, and Richard J. Orsi, eds. *Contested Eden: California before the Gold Rush*. Berkeley: University of California Press, 1998.

Haas, Lisbeth. *Conquests and Historical Identities in California, 1769–1936*. Berkeley: University of California Press, 1995.

Hackel, Steven. *Children of Coyote, Missionaries of St. Francis: Indian-Spanish Relations in Colonial California, 1769–1850*. Chapel Hill: University of North Carolina Press, 2005.

Hamalainen, Pekka. *The Comanche Empire*. New Haven, CT: Yale University Press, 2008.

———. "The Rise and Fall of Plains Horse Cultures." *Journal of American History* 90 (December 2003): 833–862.

Harmon, Alexandra. *Indians in the Making: Ethnic Relations and Indian Identities around Puget Sound*. Berkeley: University of California Press, 1998.

Hernandez, Kelly Lytle. *Migra! A History of the U.S. Border Patrol*. Berkeley: University of California Press, 2010.

Hinderaker, Eric, and Peter Mancall. *At the Edge of Empire: The Backcountry in British North America*. Baltimore: Johns Hopkins University Press, 2003.

Hine, Robert V., and John Mack Faragher. *The American West: A New Interpretive History*. New Haven, CT: Yale University Press, 2000.

Hsu, Madeline. *Dreaming of Gold, Dreaming of Home: Transnationalism and Migration between the United States and South China, 1882–1943*. Stanford, CA: Stanford University Press, 2000.

Hurtado, Albert. *Border Lord: Herbert Bolton, the West, and American History*. Berkeley: University of California Press, 2011.

———. *Intimate Frontiers: Sex, Gender, and Culture in Old California*. Albuquerque: University of New Mexico Press, 1999.

———. *John Sutter: A Life on the North American Frontier*. Norman: University of Oklahoma Press, 2006.

Hyde, Anne F. *An American Vision: Far Western Landscape and American Culture, 1820–1920*. New York: New York University Press, 1990.

Igler, David. "Diseased Goods: Global Exchanges in the Eastern Pacific Basin, 1770–1850." *American Historical Review* 109 (June 2004): 693–719.

———. *Industrial Cowboys: Miller and Lux and the Transformation of the Far West, 1850–1920*. Berkeley: University of California Press, 2001.

Jacobs, Margaret D. *White Mother to a Dark Race: Settler Colonialism, Maternalism, and the Removal of Indigenous Children in the American West and Australia, 1880–1940*. Lincoln: University of Nebraska Press, 2009.

Jacoby, Karl. *Shadows at Dawn: A Borderlands Massacre and the Violence of History*. New York: Penguin, 2008.

Jameson, Elizabeth, and Susan Armitage, eds. *Writing the Range: Race, Class, and Culture in the Women's West*. Norman: University of Oklahoma Press, 1997.

Johnson, Benjamin H. *Revolution in Texas: How a Forgotten Rebellion and Its Bloody Suppression Turned Mexicans into Americans*. New Haven, CT: Yale University Press, 2003.

Johnson, Benjamin H., and Andrew R. Graybill, eds. *Bridging National Borders in North America: Transnational and Comparative Histories*. Durham, NC: Duke University Press, 2010.

Johnson, Marilynn S. *The Second Gold Rush: Oakland and the East Bay in World War II*. Berkeley: University of California Press, 1993.

Johnson, Susan L. *Roaring Camp: A Social History of the California Gold Rush*. New York: W. W. Norton, 2000.

Josephy, Alvin M., Jr., ed. *Lewis and Clark through Indian Eyes*. New York: Knopf, 2006.

Keirnan, Ben. *Blood and Soil: A World History of Genocide and Extermination from Sparta to Darfur*. New Haven, CT: Yale University Press, 2007.

Klein, Kerwin L. *Frontiers of Historical Imagination: Narrating the European Conquest of Native America, 1890–1990*. Berkeley: University of California Press, 1997.

Kropp, Phoebe S. *California Vieja: Culture and Memory in a Modern American Place*. Berkeley: University of California Press, 2006.

Kurashige, Scott. *The Shifting Grounds of Race: Black and Japanese Americans in the Making of Multiethnic Los Angeles*. Princeton, NJ: Princeton University Press, 2008.

Lightfoot, Kent G. *Indians, Missionaries, and Merchants: The Legacy of Colonial Encounters on the California Frontier*. Berkeley: University of California Press, 2005.

Limerick, Patricia N. *The Legacy of Conquest: The Unbroken Past of the American West*. New York: W. W. Norton, 1987.

Limerick, Patricia, Clyde Milner, and Charles Rankin, eds. *Trails: Toward a New Western History*. Lawrence: University Press of Kansas, 1991.

Lotchin, Roger. *The Bad City in the Good War: San Francisco, Los Angeles, Oakland, and San Diego*. Bloomington: Indiana University Press, 2003.

Mann, Charles C. *1491: New Revelations of the Americas before Columbus*. New York: Knopf, 2005.

McGuinness, Aims. *Path of Empire: Panama and the California Gold Rush*. Ithaca, NY: Cornell University Press, 2008.

Merrill, Karen R. *Public Lands and Political Meaning: Ranchers, the Government, and the Property between Them*. Berkeley: University of California Press, 2002.

Milner, Clyde, Carol O'Connor, and Martha Sandweiss, eds. *The Oxford History of the American West*. New York: Oxford University Press, 1994.

Mitchell, Lee C. *Westerns: Making the Man in Fiction and Films*. Chicago: University of Chicago Press, 1996.

Monroy, Douglas. *Thrown among Strangers: The Making of Mexican Culture in Frontier California*. Berkeley: University of California Press, 1990.

Montoya, Maria. *Translating Property: The Maxwell Land Grant and the Conflict over Land in the American West, 1840–1900*. Berkeley: University of California Press, 2002.

Murrin, John. "Beneficiaries of Catastrophe: The English Colonies in America." In Eric Foner, ed., *The New American History*, 3–23. Philadelphia: Temple University Press, 1990.

Nicolaides, Becky M. *My Blue Heaven: Life and Politics in the Working-Class Suburbs of Los Angeles, 1920–1965*. Chicago: University of Chicago Press, 2002.

Nobles, Gregory H. *American Frontiers: Cultural Encounters and Continental Conquest*. New York: Hill and Wang, 1997.

Nugent, Walter. *Habits of Empire: A History of American Expansion*. New York: Knopf, 2008.

———. *Into the West: The Story of Its People*. New York: Knopf, 1999.

Ostler, Jeffrey. *The Plains Sioux and U.S. Colonialism from Lewis and Clark to Wounded Knee*. New York: Cambridge University Press, 2004.

Pascoe, Peggy. *What Comes Naturally: Miscegenation Law and the Making of Race in America*. New York: Oxford University Press, 2009.

Peck, Gunther. *Reinventing Free Labor: Padrones and Immigrant Workers in the North American West, 1880–1930*. New York: Cambridge University Press, 2000.

Pomeroy, Earl. *The American Far West in the Twentieth Century*. New Haven, CT: Yale University Press, 2008.

Prescott, Cynthia C. *Gender and Generation on the Far Western Frontier*. Tucson: University of Arizona Press, 2007.

Pubols, Louise. *The Father of All: The de la Guerra Family, Power, and Patriarchy in Mexican California*. Berkeley: University of California Press, 2010.

Resendez, Andres. *Changing National Identities at the Frontier: Texas and New Mexico, 1800–1850*. New York: Cambridge University Press, 2005.

Richards, Leonard L. *The California Gold Rush and the Coming of the Civil War*. New York: Knopf, 2007.

Richter, Daniel. *Facing East from Indian Country: A Native History of Early America*. Cambridge, MA: Harvard University Press, 2001.

Robb, James J., and William E. Riebsame, eds. *Atlas of the New West: Portrait of a Changing Region*. New York: W. W. Norton, 1997.

Roberts, Brian. *American Alchemy: The California Gold Rush and Middle Class Culture*. Chapel Hill: University of North Carolina Press, 2000.

Roche, Jeff, ed. *The Political Culture of the New West*. Lawrence: University Press of Kansas, 2008.

Rohrbough, Malcolm J. *Days of Gold: The California Gold Rush and the American Nation*. Berkeley: University of California Press, 1997.

———. *Trans-Appalachian Frontier: People, Societies, and Institutions, 1775–1850*. Bloomington: Indiana University Press, 2008.

Ronda, James P. *Lewis and Clark among the Indians*. Lincoln: University of Nebraska Press, 1984.

Rothman, Hal K. *Devil's Bargains: Tourism in the Twentieth-Century American West*. Lawrence: University Press of Kansas, 1998.

Sanchez, George J. *Becoming Mexican American: Ethnicity, Culture, and Identity in Chicano Los Angeles, 1900–1945*. New York: Oxford University Press, 1993.

Sandos, James A. *Converting California: Indians and Franciscans in the Missions*. New Haven, CT: Yale University Press, 2008.

Sandweiss, Martha A. *Print the Legend: Photography and the American West.* New Haven, CT: Yale University Press, 2002.

Scharff, Virginia. *Twenty Thousand Roads: Women, Movement, and the West.* Berkeley: University of California Press, 2002.

Scharff, Virginia, and Carolyn Brucken. *Home Lands: How Women Made the West.* Berkeley: University of California Press, 2010.

Self, Robert O. *American Babylon: Race and the Struggle for Postwar Oakland.* Princeton, NJ: Princeton University Press, 2003.

Slaughter, Thomas P. *Exploring Lewis and Clark: Reflections on Men and Wilderness.* New York: Knopf, 2003.

Slotkin, Richard. *Gunfighter Nation: The Myth of the Frontier in Twentieth-Century America.* New York: Athaneum, 1992.

Smith, Sherry L. *Reimagining Indians: Native Americans through Anglo Eyes, 1880–1940.* New York: Oxford University Press, 2000.

Starr, Kevin. *California: A History.* New York: Modern Library, 2005.

Tate, Michael L. *Indians and Emigrants: Encounters on the Overland Trail.* Norman: University of Oklahoma Press, 2006.

Taylor, Alan. *American Colonies: The Settling of North America.* New York: Penguin, 2001.

Taylor, Quintard. *In Search of the Racial Frontier: African Americans in the American West, 1528–1990.* New York: W. W. Norton, 1998.

Truett, Samuel. *Fugitive Landscapes: The Forgotten History of the U.S.-Mexico Borderlands.* New Haven, CT: Yale University Press, 2006.

Truett, Samuel, and Elliott Young, eds. *Continental Crossroads: Remapping U.S.-Mexico Borderlands History.* Durham: Duke University Press, 2004.

Turner, Frederick Jackson. *The Frontier in American History.* New York: Henry Holt, 1920.

———. *Rise of the New West, 1819–1829.* New York: Harper and Brothers, 1906.

Unruh, John D. *The Plains Across: The Overland Emigrants and the Trans-Mississippi West, 1840–1860.* Champaign: University of Illinois Press, 1979.

Varzally, Allison. *Making a Non-White America: Californians Coloring outside Ethnic Lines, 1925–1955.* Berkeley: University of California Press, 2008.

Warren, Louis. *Buffalo Bill's America: William Cody and the Wild West Show*. New York: Knopf, 2005.

Weber, David J. *Barbaros: Spaniards and Their Savages in the Age of Enlightenment*. New Haven: Yale University Press, 2005.

———. *The Spanish Frontier in North America*. New Haven, CT: Yale University Press, 1994.

West, Elliott. *The Contested Plains: Indians, Goldseekers, and the Rush to Colorado*. Lawrence: University Press of Kansas, 1998.

White, Richard. *"It's Your Misfortune and None of My Own": A New History of the American West*. Norman: University of Oklahoma Press, 1991.

———. *The Middle Ground: Indians, Empires, and Republics in the Great Lakes Region, 1650–1815*. New York: Cambridge University Press, 1991.

Wild, Mark. *Street Meeting: Multiethinic Neighborhoods in Early Twentieth-Century Los Angeles*. Berkeley: University of California Press, 2005.

Worster, Donald. *Under Western Skies: Nature and History in the American West*. New York: Oxford University Press, 1992.

Wrobel, David, and Michael Steiner, eds. *Many Wests: Place, Culture, and Regional Identity*. Lawrence: University Press of Kansas, 1997.